KB037797

Happy House

Contents

Syllabus 4

How to Use This Book 6

Picture Description

Unit 01	It Is a Happy Sunny Day	9
Unit 02	Do Not Touch!	13
Unit 03	Where Is the Cafeteria?	17
Unit 04	What Is This For?	21
Unit 05	They Are Similar but Different	25

Picture Discussion

Unit 06	Imagine This!	29
Unit 07	I Would Rather Choose This	33
Unit 08	She Needs Some Advice	37
Unit 09	What Do You Know about It?	41
Unit 10	This Happened Yesterday	45

Unit 11	We Met at the School Yard	49
Unit 12	Tell Me How to Make Milk Tea	53
Unit 13	Why Is the Boy Sleeping?	57

Story Making

| Unit 14 | What Happened? | 61 |
| Unit 15 | Let's Tell a Story! | 65 |

Debate

| Unit 16 | She Was Mean to Cinderella | 69 |

Talk Some More 1 ⋯⋯⋯⋯⋯⋯⋯⋯⋯⋯⋯⋯⋯⋯⋯⋯ 74

Talk Some More 2 ⋯⋯⋯⋯⋯⋯⋯⋯⋯⋯⋯⋯⋯⋯⋯⋯ 76

Syllabus

Unit	Title	Talking About	Example
01	It Is a Happy Sunny Day	pictures	• There are four trees in front of the house. In the garden, a man is watering the plants. It is a sunny day. It is a happy picture.
02	Do Not Touch!	signs and rules	• Do not take photos. • You should be quiet.
03	Where Is the Cafeteria?	directions	• The cafeteria is on the third floor. Go up the stairs. Turn left and go straight. It is on your left. You can't miss it.
04	What Is This For?	objects	• I draw or write with pencils. They are made of wood and lead. We can see pencils at home, school, and work.
05	They Are Similar but Different	similarities and differences	• The lemon is yellow. The banana is yellow too. But one is sour and the other is sweet.
06	Imagine This!	possible or impossible situations	• I would like superpowers. • I would wish for a lot of computer games.
07	I Would Rather Choose This	preferences	• I would rather have only daytime. • I would rather have only nighttime.
08	She Needs Some Advice	advice	• Why don't you hide the bag? • You should tell her not to take your things.

Unit	Title	Talking About	Example
09	What Do You Know about It?	facts and opinions	• Rabbits have a short tail and long ears. • I think rabbits are the best animals because they are cute.
10	This Happened Yesterday	the past (what, when)	• I fell off my bike yesterday. I hurt my knee. • Last weekend, I fell off my bike. I broke my wrist.
11	We Met at the School Yard	the past (who, where, why)	• On my first day of school, my mom walked with me to school. I was nervous because everything was new to me.
12	Tell Me How to Make Milk Tea	instructions	• First, boil the water. Second, put the tea bag in a cup. Third, pour the hot water and wait. Last, remove the tea bag and add milk and sugar.
13	Why Is the Boy Sleeping?	causes and effects	• The boy went to bed too late, so he is sleeping in class. • The boy is sleeping in class because he went to bed too late.
14	What Happened?	predictions	• I think some little mice made the shoes. • Maybe someone brought new shoes to help the shoemaker.
15	Let's Tell a Story!	sequences	• First, two boys are playing in the ocean. Then, they see a shark. Next, they get out of the water. Finally, they call out, "Shark!"
16	She Was Mean to Cinderella	opinions on fairy tales	• I agree because the stepmother was so mean to her. • I disagree because she is a good girl.

How to Use This Book

This section is an introduction to the unit and grabs the attention of the students. It has a focus picture followed by three questions. The questions are either comprehension or conversational and are designed to get students talking straight away. Some of the questions act as a springboard to the rest of the unit.

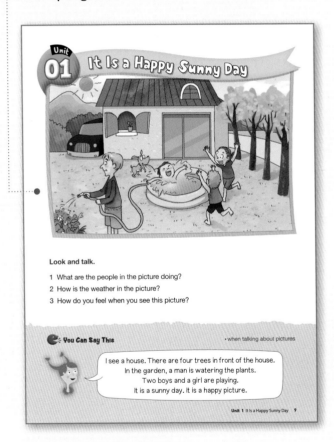

You Can Say This

You Can Say This

This part is directly related to some of the questions above. It gives the students key or example phrases and sentences used throughout the unit.

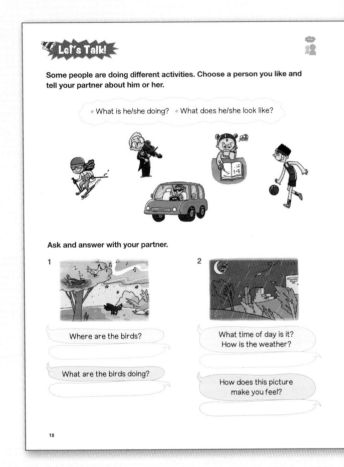

Let's Talk!

This section has two parts. The first part is designed as a conversation. It is a fun way for the students to answer a specific question as they may choose one or two answers from a selection of several choices. The second part allows the students to look at mini pictures and answer questions checking their comprehension and giving them a chance to speak.

Things Around You

Flip a coin and move along the board. When you land on each space, say two things about the object.   +1   +2

Start

Spot the Differences

Work in pairs. Find the differences between the two pictures as fast as you can and tell your partner. The winner is the one who finds the most differences.

24

12

Speak Out!

Say what you can see. Then, talk about how you feel about the pictures.

1

2

Unit 1 It Is a Happy Sunny Day **11**

Speak Out!

This section is a group or class activity. It has one question and two large pictures. Each of the pictures has enough material for groups to generate different answers.

Fun Activities

This section allows the students to reinforce or expand their speaking in a fun way. Each unit has activities such as bingo, spot the differences, information gap, find a friend, and a board game. The students can relax and have fun while using English.

★ **Review Test · Teaching Materials**
(Teacher's guide with answers, Powerpoint tool):
free download at www.ihappyhouse.co.kr

Unit 01
It Is a Happy Sunny Day

Look and talk.

1 What are the people in the picture doing?

2 How is the weather in the picture?

3 How do you feel when you see this picture?

 You Can Say This

• when talking about pictures

> I see a house. There are four trees in front of the house.
> In the garden, a man is watering the plants.
> Two boys and a girl are playing.
> It is a sunny day. It is a happy picture.

Let's Talk!

Some people are doing different activities. Choose a person you like and tell your partner about him or her.

> ✦ What is he/she doing? ✦ What does he/she look like?

Ask and answer with your partner.

1

> Where are the birds?

>

> What are the birds doing?

>

2

> What time of day is it?
> How is the weather?

>

> How does this picture
> make you feel?

>

Say what you can see. Then, talk about how you feel about the pictures.

1

2

Spot the Differences

Work in pairs. Find the differences between the two pictures as fast as you can and tell your partner. The winner is the one who finds the most differences.

Unit 02

Do Not Touch!

Look and talk.

1 Where are the people in the picture?

2 What do the signs mean?

3 Have you seen any of the signs in other places?

 You Can Say This

• when talking about signs and rules

- Do not touch.
- Do not take photos.
- You should not run.
- You should be quiet.

Let's Talk!

Which rules do you like in school? Choose two rules and talk with your partner.

✶ What should we do in school?

Ask and answer with your partner.

1

What shouldn't people do when they see this sign?

Where can we see this sign?

2

What does this sign mean?

Where have you seen this sign?

Speak Out!

Choose one person and say what he or she is doing wrong. Then, talk about what you would say to him or her.

1

2

Signs Are Everywhere

Flip a coin and move along the board. When you land on each space, say what the sign means.

+1 (10) +2

Where Is the Cafeteria?

Look and talk.

1 What rooms can you see in the picture?

2 Where is the cafeteria?

3 How can the students get to the cafeteria?

 You Can Say This

• when talking about how to get to a place

> The cafeteria is on the third floor.
> Go up the stairs. Turn left and go straight.
> It is on your left. You can't miss it.

Let's Talk!

You are at a shopping mall. Choose two places you want to visit and ask your partner where they are.

⋆ Where is this place?

Ask and answer with your partner.

1

What is next to the
train station?

How can I get to the
post office?

2

What do you see
in the picture?

How can I get to the
bookstore?

Speak Out!

Choose one place and tell your classmates how to get there. They will guess where you are going.

1

2

• Into the Forest Maze •

Work in pairs. Choose Little Red Riding Hood or Wolf. Then, take turns giving directions to Grandma's house. The winner is the first one who arrives at Grandma's house.

What Is This For?

Look and talk.

1 Where can you find these items?

2 Which one do you write with?

3 What are pencils made of?

 You Can Say This

• when talking about objects

I draw or write with pencils.
They are long and thin. They are hard.
They are made of wood and lead.
We can see pencils at home, school, and work.

Let's Talk!

Let's look in the bathroom! Choose an item and ask your partner what he or she uses it to do.

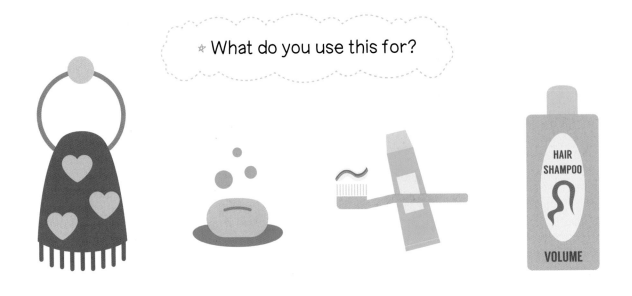

✦ What do you use this for?

Ask and answer with your partner.

1

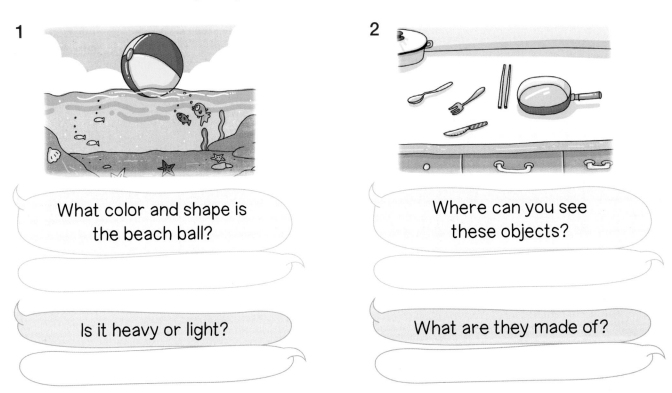

What color and shape is the beach ball?

Is it heavy or light?

2

Where can you see these objects?

What are they made of?

22

Speak Out!

Choose one object and say two things about it. Your classmates will guess which object you are talking about.

1

2

Things Around You

Flip a coin and move along the board. When you land on each space, say two things about the object.

+1 (coin) (coin) +2

They Are Similar but Different

Look and talk.

1 What fruits can you see in the picture?

2 What color are they?

3 How do they taste?

 You Can Say This

• when talking about how things are similar or different

> The lemon is yellow. The banana is yellow too.
> They are both fruits.
> But one is sour and the other is sweet.

Let's compare vehicles! Choose two vehicles and ask your partner about how they are different.

☆ How are the vehicles different?

Ask and answer with your partner.

1

What is similar about
the twin sisters?

What is different about
the twin sisters?

2

What are the people doing?

Where are they watching
the game?

Speak Out!

Choose two animals or flags and say what is similar or different about them.

1

2

How Are They Different?

Work in pairs. Choose a picture and take turns saying one sentence about it.
If what your partner says is different from your picture, circle the part.
The winner is the first one who has five circles.

Player 1

Player 2

Imagine This!

Look and talk.

1 What is happening in the picture?

2 What does the girl want to get?

3 Imagine you have a magic lamp. What would you wish for?

 You Can Say This   • when talking about possible or impossible situations

- I would like superpowers.
- I would wish for a lot of computer games.

Imagine a monster is chasing you. Choose what you would do and tell your partner.

✷ What would you do?

Ask and answer with your partner.

1

Why is the toy special?

Imagine you have a talking robot. What would you do with it?

2

Imagine you can turn into an animal. Which animal would you choose?

Why did you choose that animal?

Speak Out!

Talk about what is happening. Then, imagine you are the boy or girl and talk about what you would do.

1

2

What Would You Do?

Flip a coin and move along the board. When you land on each space, imagine that happens to you and say what you would do.

+1   +2

Start

You break your dad's glasses.

You see a spider in your room.

You are lost.

You want to play, but you have homework.

You don't like fish but your mom cooks fish.

You meet a bear in the forest.

Your friend cheats from your test.

Your tooth falls out at school.

You find money on the street.

Finish

You see a house on fire.

Your bag is missing.

Miss a Turn

You get bad grades.

You can't sleep at night.

I Would Rather Choose This

Look and talk.

1 What can you see in the picture?

2 Would you rather have only daytime or only nighttime?

3 Imagine there is no more daytime. What would you do?

 You Can Say This

• when talking about what you prefer

• I would rather have only daytime. I could play all the time.
• I would rather have only nighttime. It would be fun to play in the dark.

Your mom asks you to help her with chores. Choose one you would rather do and tell your partner.

✴ What would you rather do?

Ask and answer with your partner.

1

What is happening
in the picture?

Would you rather eat
carrots or broccoli
for one whole day?

2

Would you rather be
super smart or super strong?

Would you rather be
super strong or super fast?

Speak Out!

In the first picture, talk about who you would rather be and what you would do. In the second picture, talk about which time you would rather go to and what you would do.

1

2

Would You Rather

Flip a coin and move along the board. When you land on each space, say what you would rather choose and why.

+1 (coin) (coin) +2

Start

have
three eyes
or
three arms

have no teeth
or
no hair

be a dad/mom
or
a child

watch
a scary movie
or
a sad movie

live on the moon
or
in a jungle

live without
a TV
or
a computer

be a chef
or
a teacher

live with
City Mouse
or
Country Mouse

have
a pet whale
or
a pet pig

never eat
pizza again
or
never eat
chicken again

turn purple
or
become small
when you lie

have a brother
or
a sister

have
a broken arm
or
a broken leg

Finish

She Needs Some Advice

Look and talk.

1 How does the girl in the picture look?

2 Why do you think she feels that way?

3 She wants to make sure it doesn't happen again. What would you say to her?

 You Can Say This • when talking about what to do

- Why don't you hide the bag?
- Why don't you tell your parents about her?
- You should tell her not to take your things.

Let's Talk!

What kinds of problems do you have? Choose and tell your partner.

✫ What is your problem?

Ask and answer with your partner.

1

What is the girl's problem?

Tell her what she should do.

2

What is the boy's problem?

Tell him what he should do.

Speak Out!

Talk about what is happening. Then, talk about what the boy or girl should do.

1

2

What Should I Do?

Flip a coin and move along the board. When you land on each space, give advice to fit the problem.

+1 (coin) (10 coin) +2

Start

I want to lose weight.

I want to speak English well.

I'm always late for school.

My cat is sick.

I get a low score on a science test.

I feel sad.

My parents always read my text messages.

My friend is angry with me.

I'm bored.

I have a toothache.

I'm going to the beach, but I can't swim.

I can't remember what my homework is.

My bedroom is very cold at night.

Finish

What Do You Know about It?

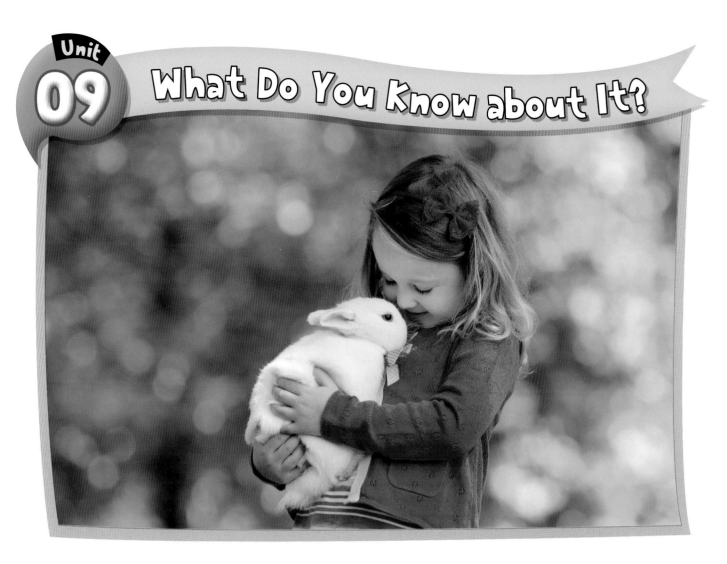

Look and talk.

1 What can you see in the picture?

2 What do you know about rabbits?

3 Do you think rabbits are the best animals? If yes, why do you think so?

 You Can Say This

• when talking about facts and opinions

- Rabbits have a short tail and long ears. They eat carrots.
- I think rabbits are the best animals because they are cute. They are also very quiet.

What school subjects do you like? Choose two subjects and ask your partner.

> ✦ What do you think about this class?

music　　English　　math　　art　　science

Ask and answer with your partner.

1
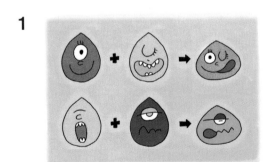

> What colors make orange?
> What colors make green?

> What is your favorite color?
> Why do you like it?

2

> What do these donuts look like?

> What do you think
> about donuts?

Say what you can see. Then, talk about what you think about the pictures.

1

2

• Fact and Opinion Bingo •

Work in pairs. Take turns saying the number of the picture. When the number is red, say something that is true about it. When the number is green, say what you think about it. Circle the pictures you and your partner say.
The winner is the first one who has four circles in a row and calls out, "Bingo!"

👆 Player 1   👉 Player 2 goes to page 78.

This Happened Yesterday

Look and talk.

1 What is happening in the picture?

2 What did the boy hurt?

3 Have you ever fallen off your bike? When was it? What happened?

 You Can Say This • when talking about what happened in the past (what, when)

• I fell off my bike yesterday. I hurt my knee.
• Last weekend, I fell off my bike. I broke my wrist.

Let's Talk!

Sometimes embarrassing things happen. Choose one that happened to you and tell your partner.

> ✫ Have any of these happened to you? When was it?

Ask and answer with your partner.

1

What is happening
in the picture?

When you didn't clean your
room, what did your mom do?

2

What is happening
in the picture?

When your friends wanted to
do something you don't like,
what did you do?

Talk about what is happening. Then, talk about when that happened to you and what you did at that time.

1

2

What Did You Do?

Flip a coin and move along the board. When you land on each space, say what you did at that time.

+1 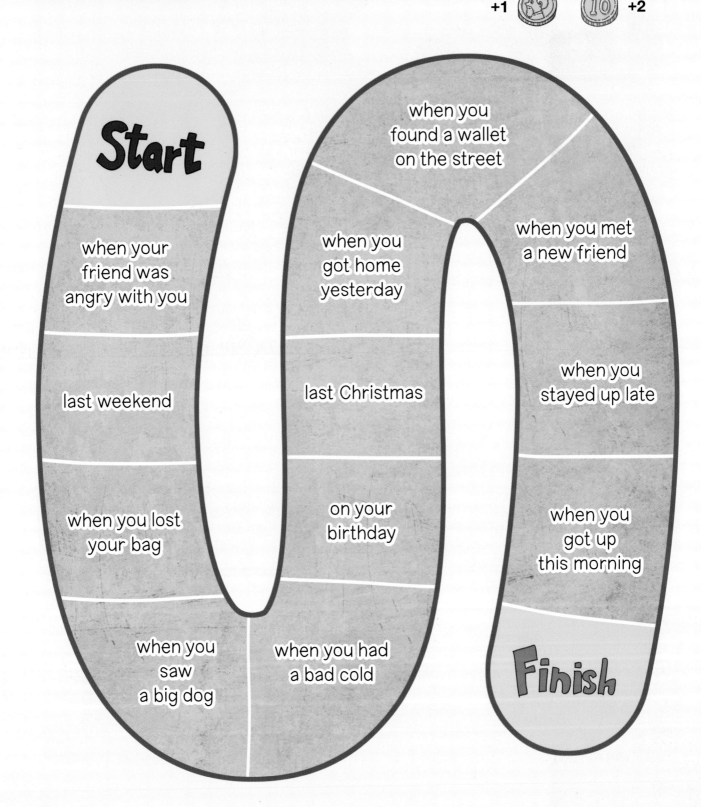 +2

Start

when your friend was angry with you

last weekend

when you lost your bag

when you saw a big dog

when you had a bad cold

on your birthday

last Christmas

when you got home yesterday

when you found a wallet on the street

when you met a new friend

when you stayed up late

when you got up this morning

Finish

We Met at the School Yard

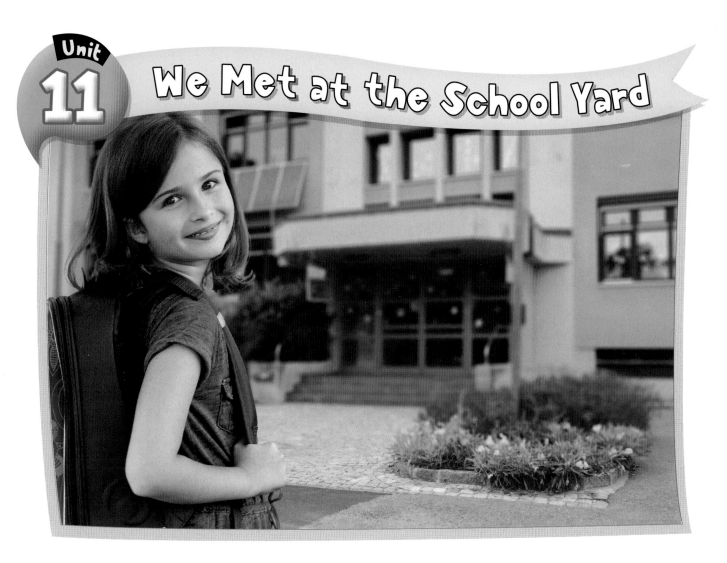

Look and talk.

1 What is the girl in the picture doing?

2 Do you remember your first day of elementary school? Who did you go with?

3 What did you do on your first day of school?

 You Can Say This   • when talking about what happened in the past (who, where, why)

> On my first day of school,
> my mom walked with me to school.
> I met my classmates at the school yard.
> I was nervous because everything was new to me.

Let's Talk!

Have you seen any of these in person? Choose all and tell your partner.

✻ Where did you see this?

Ask and answer with your partner.

1

What is happening
in the picture?

Have you had a fight with
someone? Who was it?

2

What are the people doing?

Have you gone camping?
Why did you like it
or not like it?

Speak Out!

Choose one item or type of weather and talk about your memories of it.

1

2

Find a Friend!

Ask your classmates if they did these activities last week. If they did, ask him or her to write their last names in the box. The winner is the one who has the most names.

How to play

Q Did you <u>go to a fastfood restaurant</u> last week?

A Yes, I did. ➡ Ask the following question(Who did you go with?).

A No, I didn't. ➡ Ask another classmate.

Did you … last week?

Who did you go with?

Where did you go?

Why did you go there?

Who did you go with?

Where did you play?

Why did you cry?

Who did you eat with?

Where did you watch it?

Why did you go there?

Look and talk.

1 What can you see in the picture?

2 What can you make with these things?

3 Do you know how to make a cup of milk tea?

 You Can Say This   • when talking about how to do something step by step

First, boil the water.
Second, put the tea bag in a cup.
Third, pour the hot water and wait.
Last, remove the tea bag and add milk and sugar.

Let's make the steps to show how to do two simple things! Choose and ask your partner about the last step.

☆ What is the last thing you do to draw/make this?

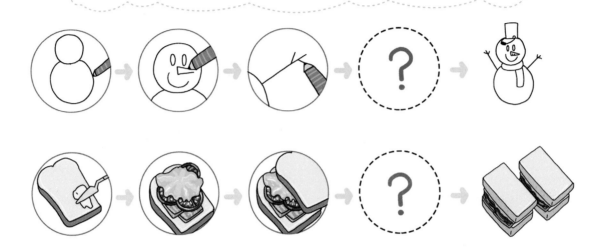

Ask and answer with your partner.

1

What is the boy doing?

How do you get dressed?

2

What is the boy doing?

How do you brush your teeth?

Think about how to make a Christmas card or ramen. Then, say one sentence each in the correct order to make the steps.

1

2

Relay Race

Stand in lines. The person at the front will say the first step for the activity. Then, the next person will repeat what they heard and say the second step. Continue until your line completes all the steps. The winner is the first line that finishes. Take turns and change orders.

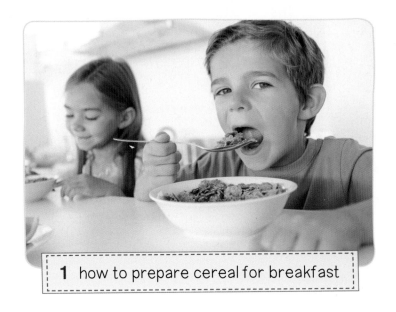

1 how to prepare cereal for breakfast

2 how to boil eggs

3 how to wash your hands

Why Is the Boy Sleeping?

Look and talk.

1 What is happening in the pictures?

2 Why is the boy sleeping in class?

3 Have you ever fallen asleep in class? Why?

  You Can Say This   • when talking about why something happens and what happens

> • The boy went to bed too late, so he is sleeping in class.
> • The boy is sleeping in class because he went to bed too late.

Let's Talk!

These events happen with the weather. Choose and tell your partner about it.

☆ What is happening?   ☆ Why is this happening?

Ask and answer with your partner.

1

What is happening
in the picture?

Why is this happening?

2

What are the baby and
the dog doing?

What will happen?

58

Speak Out!

In the first picture, say one sentence each about what is happening and why that is happening. In the second picture, say one sentence each about what happened and what is happening.

Spot the Differences

Work in pairs. Find the differences between the two pictures as fast as you can and tell your partner the differences in cause and effect. The winner is the one who finds the most differences.

Look and talk.

1 What is happening in the first two pictures?

2 What is happening in the last two pictures?

3 Who do you think made the shoes?

You Can Say This

• when talking about what you think happened before

- • I think some little mice made the shoes.
- • I think some elves or fairies made the shoes.
- • Maybe someone brought new shoes to help the shoemaker.

The giant is chasing the boy. Choose what you think happened before and talk with your partner.

> ☆ What do you think happened before?

Ask and answer with your partner.

1 What is happening in the pictures?

2 What do you think happened in the middle picture?

Look and think about what happened in the middle picture. Then, tell your own story by using the pictures.

What Happened to Them?

**Make groups. Read each story and answer the questions together.
Then, share the best idea from your group with your classmates.**

The girl named Little Red Riding Hood liked to visit her grandparents. They lived in an apartment across town. Little Red Riding Hood's mother asked her to take some soup and cake to her grandparents' house. "Please be careful!" her mother said. She was always worried about strangers.
Little Red Riding Hood arrived at her grandparents' house but they did not answer the door. She got in the house, and she was shocked.
A big red monster was there!

1 Why did Little Red Riding Hood visit her grandparents?

2 What did Little Red Riding Hood find at her grandparents' house?

3 What do you think happened to the grandparents?

There was a boy named Peter. He always told lies. He lied to his mother and father and everyone!
One day, Peter went to a big store. He said, "Look, there is a thief!" The police came but there was no thief. The next day, he said, "Fire! Fire!" The firemen came, but there was no fire. The next day, Peter lied again. After that Peter did not tell lies anymore. He only told the truth.

1 What did Peter do wrong?

2 What lies did Peter tell?

3 Why do you think Peter stopped telling lies?

Let's Tell a Story!

Look and talk.

1 What is happening in the first two pictures?

2 What do the boys do after they see something in the water?

3 What do the boys do last?

You Can Say This

• when telling a story in order

First, two boys are playing in the ocean.
Then, they see a shark.
Next, they get out of the water.
Finally, they call out, "Shark!"

Let's Talk!

Brian is fighting with his friend. Choose the reason you think they are fighting and tell your partner.

☆ Why do you think they are fighting?

Ask and answer with your partner.

1 Put the numbers in order and tell the story.
2 What do you think the bear said?

Make a story with your classmates by using the pictures. Choose a picture to start the story. Continue until the story is complete.

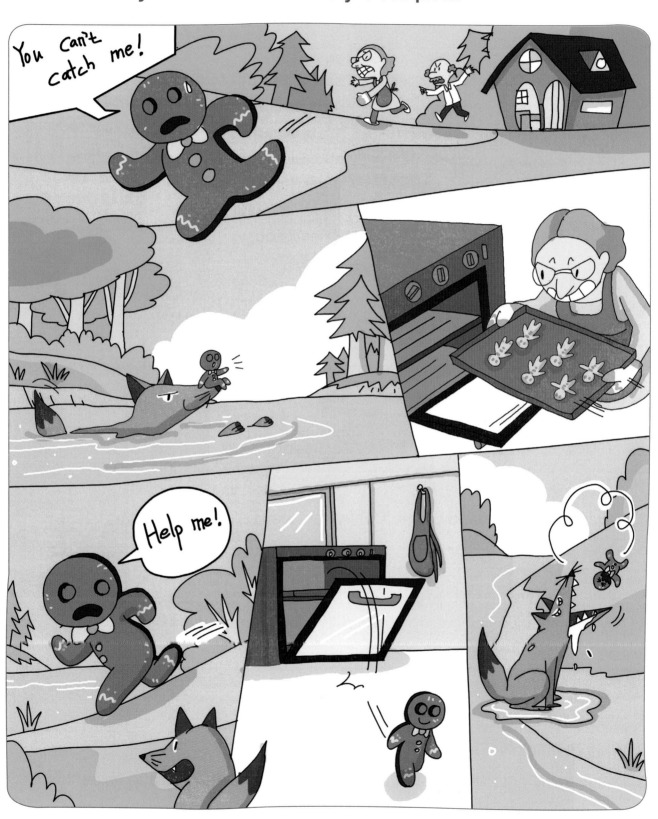

• Be the Story Maker! •

**Make groups. Read each story and answer the questions together.
Then, share the best idea from your group with your classmates.**

Lily was walking in her garden. She saw a beautiful fox beside the rose bush. The fox looked hungry, so she fed it. Then, the fox followed her to her house. She made a bed for the fox to sleep in.

The fox came to Lily's house every day. Lily always gave the fox some delicious food and they walked in her garden.

She and the fox became friends. Lily's friend saw the fox and got jealous. He wanted to be its friend, too.

1 What was the first thing that Lily did to the fox?

2 What did Lily do with the fox every day?

3 Imagine you are Lily's friend. How will you become friends with the fox? Make a plan with three steps.

It was a dark and windy night. Heavy rain was falling. Two men were riding horses on the road. One horse was white as snow and the other horse was black as night. The two men stopped on a bridge when they saw a giant blocking the way. The giant had long brown hair and bright green eyes. The two men asked, "Please let us pass."

1 Why did the two men stop on the bridge?

2 What did the giant look like?

3 Imagine you are the giant. What three steps do the men have to follow to pass?

She Was Mean to Cinderella

Look and talk.

1 What is Cinderella doing in the first picture?

2 What do you think about Cinderella's stepmother?

3 Do you think Cinderella should punish her stepmother after she marries the prince?

 You Can Say This

• when talking about your opinions

• I agree because the stepmother was so mean to her.
• I disagree because she is a good girl.

What is your favorite fairy tale? Choose and ask your partner if he or she agrees.

☆ The best fairy tale is this. Do you agree?

Pinocchio

Aladdin

Peter Pan

Sleeping Beauty

Alice in Wonderland

Ask and answer with your partner.

1 What did each of the wolves do wrong?

2 Which wolf is worse?

   Tell your partner what you think and ask if he or she agrees.

Speak Out!

Say which statement you agree with and why. Write down the names of your classmates who are on the same side as you.

1

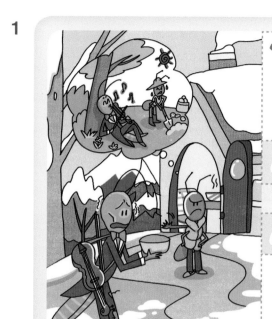

Ant is not kind.

Vs.

Ant is not bad.

2

Country Mouse should live in the city.

Vs.

Country Mouse should go back to the country.

Let's Debate!

Read and debate.

Fairy tales are fun to read.

Agree

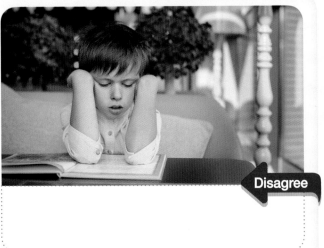

Disagree

Fairy tales need to have a happy ending.

Agree

Disagree

72

Appendices

Talk Some More 1 ——————————————————— 74

Talk Some More 2 ——————————————————— 76

Fact and Opinion Bingo `Unit 09` ———————————— 78

Talk Some More 1

Roll a die and move along the board.
Answer the questions or talk about the pictures.

Start

Find a person who has a birthday this month.

What do you use scissors for?

What is similar about penguins and eagles?

Say something that is true about polar bears.

Have you helped your friend? What did you do?

Name something made of metal.

What do you think about this hat?

Would you rather have a pet snake or a pet spider? Why?

I'm tired. What should I do?

How is the weather today?

Roll the Die Again

Imagine you found an alien in the living room. What would you do?

Go Back to Start

Why is the boy crying?

Finish

Have you ever visited another country? Where did you go?

How do you wash your hair?

Why is this happening?

Find a person who read a book yesterday.

Shout "Hello!" Three Times

Miss a Turn

How can I get to the hair salon?

When did you watch a movie?

Have you had a fight with someone? Why did you fight?

Talk Some More 2

Roll a die and move along the board.
Answer the questions or talk about the pictures.

Start

When your mom was angry with you, what did you do?

Say something that is true about apples.

Imagine you turned into your dad. What would you do?

What do you use a chair for?

Why is this happening?

What is different about penguins and eagles?

How do you make a snowman?

Did you talk on the phone yesterday? Who did you talk with?

I'm bored. What should I do?

When did you go to bed last night?

What do you use a comb for?

How do you make milk tea?

What do you think about your teacher?

Ask Quest

Move Ahead 2 Spaces

Name two things made of wood.

Say what you see and what you think about this picture.

What will happen to him?

Go Back to Start

Would you rather have a new phone or a new computer? Why?

Should Little Red Hen share the bread with her friends?

What do you think about swimming?

Imagine you can be anyone for a day. Who would you be?

Shout "Hurray!" Three Times

Finish

• Fact and Opinion Bingo •

Work in pairs. Take turns saying the number of the picture. When the number is red, say something that is true about it. When the number is green, say what you think about it. Circle the pictures you and your partner say.
The winner is the first one who has four circles in a row and calls out, "Bingo!"

Player 2

Memo

Memo